Rob Versus The Morons

Overcoming Idiotic Customers with Wit, Sarcasm and a Take No Bullshit Attitude

Rob Anspach

Rob Versus The Morons

Overcoming Idiotic Customers with
Wit, Sarcasm and a Take No Bullshit Attitude

Copyright © 2020 by Anspach Media
Cover Design by: Freddy Solis
Cover Photo by: Gustavo Fernández, www.gustavofernandez.com

All rights reserved. No part of this book may be reproduced or transmitted in any form or by any means without written permission from the author.

ISBN 13: 978-1-7324682-3-8

Printed in USA

Disclaimer: Oh yes, we must have a disclaimer…it makes the lawyers happy. The author has spent a lifetime using sarcasm as a means to grow his business. He shares interactions in this book that you may or may not agree with, his actions and communications are contrary to what most customer service gurus teach. But, it works for him and could work for you too, although highly doubtful.

Table of Contents

Introduction by: Rob Anspach	9
Chapter 1 – The First Lessons	11
Chapter 2 – We Are Google	21
Chapter 3 – Not Holding My Breath	27
Chapter 4 – You Want Me To Write What?	39
Chapter 5 – Endless Wonder	45
Chapter 6 – The Closer	53
Chapter 7 – Getting Reported	59
Chapter 8 – Just Pay Me	69
Chapter 9 – X Plus $10,000	79
Chapter 10 – Chief Instigator	87
Chapter 11 – Staying Loyal	93
Chapter 12 – Trust Us	109
Chapter 13 – The F-You Awards	117
Chapter 14 – Stupid Is As Stupid Does	127
About The Author	133
Resources	134

"The universe is made up of protons, neutrons, electrons and unfortunately…morons."

What People Are Saying

"Whoever coined the phrase 'the customer is always right' was probably a customer lobbing a feebly-thrown Hail Mary pass from deep in their own end zone, backed into a corner by their own arrogance and ignorance. In this book, Rob says what many of us wish we had the balls to say. And, as long as he can keep these misguided fools on the phone, he will continue to gather evidence which proves that a portion of the business world seems to enjoy keeping its head lodged in a warm, dark place...like an ostrich that has lost its sense of smell."
- **Steve Gamlin, The Motivational Firewood™ Guy**

"If you have ever had the misfortune of dealing with incompetent customer service on the phone or online, then you must read Rob's new book which takes you in-depth into conversations with customer service representatives who have absolutely no clue what they are doing.

Reading Rob's fast-paced, story-filled book makes you feel as if you are secretly listening in on his mind-blowing conversations not only with customer service but also with business owners and entrepreneurs who don't understand what it means to play by the rules. Logic gets thrown out the window when trying to explain to a customer service rep how ridiculous it is to receive a reference number for something that no one ever takes any notes about. Equally insane is when a business owner attempts to do things their own way and expects Rob to play along.

Learn how Rob uses his sarcasm and wit to make his point over and over again. As you read along, you will say to yourself "That's exactly what happened to me the last time I was on the phone with customer service!" Do yourself a favor, get a copy of Rob's new book "Rob Versus The Morons" immediately. You'll thank me, you'll thank Rob and then you'll start searching to learn where you can get a copy of "Rob Versus The Scammers" which is even funnier." – **Gerry Oginski, Great Neck, New York**

"A brilliant read! I'm a bit of a "grammar police" myself, so the first 'story' hit home! I loved the notes at the end of each lesson! I abhor Customer Service Assistants who don't understand English, so I can identify with the sarcasm used - at times it was like you were in my head, saying my words! Be glad you don't have to deal with some CS Departments in South Africa!! You'd be able to write volumes! Some people just don't, can't or won't listen! "Other people named..." and "A Priest, A Rabbi & A President....." had me howling. I read them both twice, just for fun. A good, quick read, guaranteed to cheer you up on a grey day!"
- Sioux Gijzen, Boksburg, Gauteng South, Africa

"If you want a word duel, see Rob Anspach! Just expect to lose, especially if you refuse to engage in a "sensible" conversation. Rob shares his trials and tribulations with customers and customer service people all over the world, and leaves them reeling in his wake. If you want a gift of humor for that special someone, I highly recommend "Rob vs the Morons"!"
-Laura Toogood, Toronto, Ontario Canada

"Reading any book in the "Rob versus..." series is a master class in how to do business effectively and probably profitably. It's also very instructive in how not to be the customer from Hell. Rob don't play that. I've enjoyed every book I've gotten from him, as Rob delivers excellent content." - **Jocelyn Stewart Bagley**

"If you only have the time to read one book this year your time will be well spent breezing through Rob's new book "Rob Versus the Morons". And, if all you learn is how not to be a ... well, then your time will be well spent. You'll find Rob's story telling entertaining and informative. And, even if you are not into marketing, you'll find that Rob's most important rule applies to any profession. Master it and success will follow." – **David W. Holub, Merrillville, Indiana**

"A super fun read."
– **Lee Milteer,** Author of "Success Is An Inside Job"

"In my earliest days as an entrepreneur, over 15 years ago, I learned the hard way how important it is to "Say NO To Success!" They don't teach this in Business Building 101 - but the more you turn down bad-fit prospects and pay attention to red flags (not to mention your gut feelings, even if the deal appears to check off all the boxes), the more successful your business will be and the more ideal-fit prospects you will attract. Rob Anspach delivers a highly sarcastic yet poignant view, combining humor with extreme-case examples that provide an important reminder why you must set a high expectations bar not only for yourself, but also for those you choose to work with, in order to have a prosperous and profitable business you will enjoy."
- **Adam Hommey, Speaker • Author • Consultant • Trainer**

"It's refreshing to find a book that puts a grin on your face from the moment you read the table of contents. Coupled with a powerful insight that success follows being your authentic self, even when including a dark humor and sarcasm, the lessons throughout this book shed light on many basic elements for online business management. Rob cuts right to the chase with content that is both educational and hilarious. The book should rank on just his introduction to analytical, psychological, and emotional marketing, that affects how we think, behave & feel. Short precise lessons. Easy to grasp. Easy to understand. Easy to relate to, making the book hard to put down, Rob demonstrates common sense knowledge with uncommon brilliance. He truly is the King of Content Creation."
– **Paula Frate,** RN Home Health Consultant ~ Education, Performance Improvement, Regulatory Compliance - Houston TX

"Rob Anspach has done it again. This latest work is brilliant, informative, and entertaining. If you only read the notes at the end of the sections, you'll learn valuable information and advice. But then you'll miss out on Rob's delicious sarcasm and wit as he navigates frustrating situations that we all encounter and only dream we could handle half as well as he does. Throughout this page-turner you'll find yourself wishing you could run your business and live your life on your own terms, as Rob does, and the good news is that -- by following Rob's lead -- you can!" - **Steve Sipress**

Rob Anspach

INTRODUCTION
By: Rob Anspach

I've spent the last 25 years of my life as an entrepreneur and I can tell you that being an entrepreneur has to be done on your terms. If that means someone views you as a jerk, a curmudgeon or even an asshole that's okay. In fact, the more I allowed my personality to shine (more like my sarcasm to be front and center) the easier it was to disqualify those who truly weren't a right fit for me.

But, before I became an entrepreneur I heard the phrase "the customer is always right" so many times I wondered why anyone would want to own a business. Then when I did become an entrepreneur, I discovered the truth. The customer is rarely right, yet they want you as the business owner to bend over and take it. Nah, that's not how I wanted to run my company.

Sure, without customers most businesses won't survive. However, as a business owner you do not have to accept every person as a customer. You can pick and choose your customers or in my case, use wit and sarcasm to weed out the undesirables.

Okay, as to my sarcasm…it became my super power. Those who thought I was funny or joking became great clients. Those who thought otherwise…well, they either didn't become clients or didn't stay clients for very long.

So the same sarcastic attitude I used to defend against fraudsters in my book "Rob Versus The Scammers" I used to field calls, texts, emails and in-person exchanges to deal with irritating and obnoxious people. Somedays it worked, somedays it didn't. But, I did it on my terms.

Now some might say, "I would never treat people like that" or "Rob how do even have a business with that kind of behavior" but, as I explained, the customer isn't always right they just don't understand your process, your thinking or they believe all services are the same. Once you set the ground rules (example: that your time is valuable, or these are our policies) then it becomes easier for expectations between you and the client to be met.

The clients who stick with me, soon realize I am one of the good guys and will treat them as family…albeit sarcastically.

Enjoy the book.

Rob Anspach
www.AnspachMedia.com

Oh, if you're curious about the photo on the cover…

I had to introduce myself at **Steve Sims Speakeasy event** (San Francisco CA - November 2019)

So I stood up and said…

"Hi, I'm Rob Anspach, the sarcastic one...
I'm a serial author, podcaster and a specialized SEO expert. I've authored, coauthored or produced 23 books in 6 years with my next book coming out soon. It's called 'Rob Versus The Morons'. And my biggest fear is being the smartest one in the room."

So there you have it…in real life, on the phone or in the book…the sarcasm never stops.

Chapter 1

The First Lessons

"...and why you will fail as an entrepreneur!"

Ignore The Rules

Rob, I have a few of your books and I noticed some grammar and punctuation changes that need to occur, may I send you my findings?

Me: What do you do for a living?

I'm a grade school teacher.

Me: And what are you doing reading my books?

I want to learn how to be an entrepreneur.

Me: First rule of being an entrepreneur...ignore the rules.

But grammar and punctuation are important.

Me: Maybe. But I've sold thousands of books and 99% of the readers don't care about my grammar or punctuation mistakes they are reading the books for the content.

Well you should really take the time to make sure they're perfect before sending your books out.

Me: And that's where you will fail as an entrepreneur.

Huh?

Me: You are too caught up in the notion that perfection equates to something...it doesn't. Good is better than perfect. A good product can start making you money right off the mark. If you waited for a product to be perfect it would never ever be released, because it wouldn't live up to your standards.

Really, name a company that operates that way.

Me: Apple, Microsoft, Disney, Facebook, YouTube, Chevrolet, Ford, shall I go on?

Oh?

Me: So are you going to send me your findings?

No, I suppose not.

Me: And there end's your first lesson.

Note: Too many entrepreneurs get hung up on the whole "got to be perfect" philosophy and won't release a product, course, book or whatever it is until it's absolutely spot on their vision. Get the product out, start making money, then when you have time go back and make improvements.

Doing The Same Things Expecting Different Results

But Rob, we were accustomed to doing things differently with the last company we worked with.

(translation: they were doing the same things every other marketer in their niche was doing)

Me: Okay and why are you reaching out to me?

Well, we need help. We need better results.

Me: Well, then the first rule of working with me is "don't question my methods"

But, your methods are...

Me: What was my first rule?

Hmm, don't question your methods

Me: Now you're catching on.

Note: The definition of insanity is doing the same thing over and over but expecting different results each time. If you hire me (or any consultant) it's because you are tired of the insanity and want something better for your business.

Forget The TV and Grow Your Business Instead

Hey Rob, I only have a budget of $300 a month for marketing, what do you suggest?

Me: Upping your budget.

Them: Not an option.

Me: Cut back on stuff you don't need.

Them: Need it all.

Me: Really?

Them: Yup.

Me: Hmm, how much do you spend on TV a month?

Them: $300 for all the channels.

Me: Do you need all the channels?

Them: Probably not, but I can't live without TV.

Me: Really? I beg to differ.

Them: I really do watch a lot of TV.

Me: Yet you want your business to do better, you want to attract more customers and you want more money in your pocket right?

Them: So you want me to get rid of the TV and spend it on marketing to grow the business?

Me: Now you're catching on.

Them: But then I might get too busy and not be able to watch my favorite programs.

Me: And?

Them: That would suck.

Me: What sucks is your attitude to growing your business, you would rather sit on your ass watching TV. than grow your business.

Them: Kind of harsh aren't you?

Me: Nope, and honestly, I cut cable about 10 years ago and stream everything. Saves me a ton of money, stops me from wasting countless hours in front of the TV and keeps me focused on growing my company.

Them: I also play video games, I bet you want me to stop playing right?

Me: You don't have to stop playing, just back off on how many hours you play them.

Them: By how much?

Me: Ugh, are listening to yourself? You value TV and video games over making money.

Them: Well they are my life.

Me: And how much do you spend per month on video games, systems and accessories?

Them: About $500 a month.

Me: Seems to me between cutting back on TV and Video games you could up your marketing budget and be on your way to creating a better life for yourself.

Them: Is there another way?

Me: Sure, get rid of the business and sit on your ass all day.

<he hung up>

Note: You have to decide what is more important….the here and now or the brighter future. Sadly, I've come across way too many entrepreneurs who focused on the now and think the future is too far off and not worth their time. Don't be that person.

Becoming The Authority In Your Niche

But Rob, my consultant says I don't need all that content.

Me: If you don't want to become the authority in what you do then yes, they are correct.

Them: But I just don't have time to produce all that content.

Me: Give me 2 hours of time per month and I'll create enough content for you for the next 30 days.

Them: Wow.

Me: Yes, Wow is right. But let me ask you, does your current consultant have a podcast? Do they post articles to their blog every week? Do they send their subscribers a daily newsletter? Do they post to their social media daily?

Them: No podcast, the last article on their website is dated January 2016, I've never received a newsletter and they only post to social maybe twice a month.

Me: Then why did you hire them?

Them: Well they seemed to know what they are doing.

Me: Well there's a big difference between seem to know and actually knowing. And that difference is what is holding you back as the authority in your niche.

Note: There are plenty of people who seem to know stuff, however, if they are telling you things that don't seem right or just don't make sense in anyway make sure you do your due diligence and check up on them. Look at what others are saying. Read reviews. Ask questions. Do research. Just because a consultant knows a thing or two, make sure it jives with your goals, and that what they teach they are actually implementing and using for themselves.

Rob Anspach

Chapter 2

We Are Google!

"Resistance Is Futile!"

When The Google Rep Can't Help

On the phone with Google (somewhere in India). I have repeated myself 10x and the person repeats everything back then wants to patronize me.

I say, "put someone else on the phone, life is too short to talk to you."

Google rep: "Mr. Robert I can help you Sir."

Me: No you can't, I had to repeat everything over and over again, now put someone else on the phone.

Google rep: Mr. Robert please bear with me.

Me: I'm done with you, find someone else, hell put the dog barking in the background on the phone I don't care.

Google rep: Sir I will find someone to help you.

{puts me on hold for 5 mins, probably looking for the dog to put on the phone}

Google rep: Sorry Sir I could not find anyone to help you.

Me: Keep looking.

{they hung up}

Even Google Needs Time To Fix Stuff

Hi Google, it's me Rob.

Google: Hi Rob.

Me: Can you fix something for me?

Google: Sure I will get my best techs on it and have it fixed in 24 hours.

Me: Thank you very much.

{27 hours later...me calling back}

Hi Google it's me Rob.

Google: I see we helped you yesterday.

Me: Yes you said your techs would have the problem solved in 24 hours and to call back if not fixed, so I'm calling back.

Google: You will have to be patient, some things take time.

Me: I get that, but if you tell me 24 hours and 27 hours later it's not fixed then it's not a question of patience it's a problem of over-promising your deliverables.

Google: We are Google!

Me: And I am Rob!

Google: What do you wish of us?

Me: An actual time that the issue will be fixed.

Google: Could take 2 weeks.

Me: So you basically did a reverse Scotty from Star Trek...instead of fixing the problem in a faster time frame you basically throw out a time frame knowing full well it won't get fixed.

Google: Scotty? I don't see him on your account.

Me: OMG...you know beam me up Scotty there is no intelligent life here?

Google: Are you saying we are dumb?

Me: Oy vey, that's not what I meant...

Google: Is there anything else we can help you with?

Me: Nope, just hoping it doesn't take 2 weeks to fix the problem.

Google: It could take up to 2 weeks. We hope not. But it could. But if it takes longer, it is what it is. Can't rush these things.

Me: So basically it'll get fixed when it gets fixed.

Google: Are you satisfied with the call today?

Me: I'll let you know in 2 weeks.

Note: Many big tech companies have contracted with foreign call centers that make it hard to actually get a straight answer. More and more consumers are becoming overly frustrated with the lack of service they receive from these so-called customer support reps. I have to deal with Google (reps) several times a month as a courtesy for my clients. And sadly, it always seems to go the same way. But, it's a great way to hone my powers of sarcasm.

Rob Anspach

Chapter 3

Not Holding My Breath

"Or volunteering for life support."

My Web Guy Said SEO Is Dead

"Hey Rob, I was told SEO is dead!"

Me: Nope.

Them: Then it's on life support.

Me: Nope.

Them: Well my buddy who builds sites says so.

Me: What's his website URL?

{Proceeds to tell me, so I look it up}

Me: Sheesh, no wonder this guy has no clue what he's doing and tells everyone SEO is dead.

Them: Really you can see that.

Me: Dude, this is what I do. And I do it every day. As soon as I scan the source code of a website I can instantly see what he's doing wrong, and boy is this guy missing out on all kinds of SEO.

Them: So no good.

Me: I feel sorry for any of his clients.

Them: Apparently he has lots of them and he tells them that SEO doesn't matter anymore.

Me: Oh it matters more now than ever.

NOTE: If your website isn't optimized properly it won't show up in the search engine results page when potential clients look for you. If you want more traffic to your page, more people calling you and more clients, then your website needs to be properly optimized.

Playing SEO Hardball

Just got off the phone with a web design company who was looking for my help with SEO. I said great I will need full admin access to each site you want me to optimize.

"*No can do*", they said, "*We don't grant access to anyone beyond our company*". So I say, "*not even your clients?*"

They reply, "*especially our clients*".

Me: But it's their website.

Them: Yes, but we don't want them screwing it up.

Me: So you basically build them something they have zero access to, can't make changes without calling you and are forced to pay you month after month after month for an asset they really don't own.

Them: Oh, they own it.

Me: No, they basically rent it.

Them: So are you going to help us with SEO?

Me: Well I need direct access.

Them: Can't you just tell us what needs fixed, where to fix it and my team can do the actual fixing?

Me: Sure, if you want to spend twice the amount of money for my services, or grant me access and let me just work my magic.

Them: Like I said, we don't grant access beyond our own company.

Me: Think of me as an extension of your company looking out for the best interest of your clients online reputation.

Them: Nope

Me: Why did you call me?

Them: We heard you're the best at SEO.

Me: Well if you want my service then I need full access, if not find another SEO guy.

Them: Okay we will let you know.

{me not holding my breath}

Note: Over the last decade I've probably had this exact conversation at least six times. Some web designers are so overly protective of their sites and would rather double charge the client then allow outside access.

Are All SEO Services The Same?

Rob, your price to optimize my website is 3x higher than what my web guy is charging me, what gives? Are you trying to rip people off?

Me: Let me answer that with a question...would you prefer to own a Ford Pinto or a Ferrari F8 Spider.

Them: Well the Ferrari of course.

Me: So if you could afford a finely tuned sports car like a Ferrari then is it really a rip off?

Them: Well, no.

Me: But me providing you a level of value that's superior to how your web guy is presently SEO'ing your site is?

Them: So are you the Ferrari?

Me: I am - and here's why. My job is to make sure your site is not only seen by the search engines but when it shows up in the results people are looking for - it's a head turner, a feeling of excitement and they say "wow, that's what I need right now."

Them: So my guy is the Pinto?

Me: Typically yes, they built you what appears to be a solid website, unfortunately it rarely shows up in search rankings, and just lingers in the far reaches of the interwebs gathering dust. Most web guys don't understand the dynamics of keywords and how to use those keywords to rank faster in the search results. They think ranking you for 3-5 industry standard keywords is the norm.

Them: So why is your method different.

Me: What makes me the Ferrari is that I don't settle for just 3-5 industry standard keywords. The way I optimize a site I could have you ranking for 30-50 or more keywords that cover the analytical (how people think), the psychological (how people behave) and the emotional (how people feel) because it's those keywords that will outrank industry terms all day long, eliminate tire kickers and attract the very client you wish to work with.

Them: When can we get started.

Note: I mention the SEO scammers in my book "Rob Versus The Scammers" and their whole premise (or promise) is to rank you for 3-5 industry standard keywords. So basically you are using the same words as all your competitors, yet you are doing nothing to attract the right audience to your website.

Cheap SEO Is Not Our Deal

Hey Rob, we are looking for someone cheap to do our SEO.

Me: How's that working out for you?

Them: Well we've been looking.

Me: Okay so why call me?

Them: Well we were hoping you'd give us a deal.

Me: Nope, keep looking.

Them: You haven't looked at our site yet.

Me: I heard all I needed.

Them: Huh?

Me: You said you are looking for cheap and immediately asked for a deal, I don't do cheap or make deals.

Them: So you aren't going to help us?

Me: What do you think?

Them: I don't know...are you?

Me: Well my prices start at XXX.

Them: Holy shit...yeah we'll need a deal.

Me: There's your answer.

Them: What? What's the answer?

Me: If I'm going to help you.

Them: I don't get it.

Me: Exactly.

Them: You aren't making sense.

Me: Look you can't afford me, so keep looking.

Them: Why didn't you just say that?

Note: The lower the price the more hassles involved. That's exactly what cheap clients offer...hassles. Understand the value you deliver and back it up with a profitable price that keeps you in business long after those cheap competitors have gone out of business.

Expecting The Best Is Expensive

Hey Rob, I Heard You're The Best.

Me: Well, I am many things, depends on who you ask.

Them: Hah, I heard from 4 people you are the best at SEO.

Me: Yes, that is one of the things I am very good at.

Them: Good I want the best.

Me: How can I help?

Them: I need my website optimized.

{Me quickly looking at site...thinking OMG, not a walk in the park by any stretch}

Me: You have a lot of content on the site.

Them: Yeah, and lots of videos too.

Me: Yes, hundreds of videos and a few hundred blog articles...and unfortunately zero optimization.

Them: Can you give me a price on fixing everything.

Me: Yup, but you're not going to like it.

Them: So you're telling me the price is going to be high.

Me: It's going to be most likely way higher than you want.

Them: Why do you say that?

Me: Several reasons (1) your site is 6 years old with a massive amount of content (2) it's going to take me time to optimize everything and (3) you're not the first person to come to me with this type of request.

Them: Oh, so you can't do it for a few hundred a month?

Me: Try a few thousand.

Them: Okay maybe I don't need the best.

Note: I see way too many website owners create content for their websites and after years wonder why it's not producing results. You would think that after a few months of getting results they would seek out help, but nope. Years go by and then they can't afford to have the content fixed. If your website isn't producing results reach to my team and we'd be glad to offer some pointers.

Rob Anspach

Chapter 4

You Want Me To Write What?

"Yeah, not today, or tomorrow, or ever!"

The Outdated Blogging Strategy Some People Still Want

Hi Rob, I see you write blog articles for clients, right?

Me: Yes.

Well, I need a series of articles written.

Me: Okay.

I would like 2 articles per month to be put on my website and optimized.

Me: Okay.

I need each article to mention my company, location and service multiple times in the articles too.

Me: Nope.

What do you mean nope?

Me: That strategy is so outdated and not recommended.

Well who is the customer? This is what I want you to do.

Me: Nope.

If you want my business then YES, you will write the articles as I want them.

Me: So basically you want me to write crap just so you can have some articles on your website.

I don't want crap. I want articles that rank.

Me: Well, that's not how you get website blog articles to rank, but it is good way to turn off every reader who tries to read those articles. What you want are basically keyword stuffed POS (*piece of shit) articles that do nothing to engage the reader.

Can you write them or not.

Me: I don't write articles like that. I do however write pieces that are educational and centered on the user experience. We don't keyword stuff articles. If that's what you want you need to call someone...

{the caller hung up}

Note: When your website blog articles receive comments from legitimate readers (not spammers) that tells the search engines your website is getting engagement. The more engagement the more chances the search engines will reward you by showing your article in searches.

Blogging Versus Social Media

Hey Rob, I don't blog because it's easier just to post to social media.

Me: Yes, I hear that a great deal. Unfortunately, the social media networks are then getting the traffic and not your website.

Them: So.

Me: Okay, but do you own Facebook or control Twitter or work at LinkedIn?

Them: What does that have to do with not blogging.

Me: Simple, when you don't control the platform you are posting to, you are relying on a 3rd party to facilitate your message. They have full control over how your message is received by an audience.

Them: What?

Me: Posting more articles on your website blog gives you control of your message and what is being seen by your audience. You can share those articles to various social platforms but you are not relying on those platforms because you don't control them. And instead of the social networks getting the traffic, now your website which you own is getting the traffic.

Them: But I need to come up with blog articles.

Me: The same content you would have shared on social media can be expanded into articles for your website.

Them: Social media is easier.

Me: Yes it is, but now your website has very little informative content that would tell a potential client why they should trust you as the authority in your niche.

Them: But they can just read what I post on my Facebook, Twitter and LinkedIn

Me: You're not understanding the importance of posting content to your own platform and that's why you are not attracting the right clients.

Note: Social media is great…but, unfortunately it takes away from the traffic your website should be receiving. The key is to get your fans, friends and followers to engage with your website by commenting and sharing your blog articles.

Rob Anspach

Chapter 5

Endless Wonder

"That's sarcasm for…I wonder when it will end."

Tracking Emails For Easier Payment

Hey Rob, I didn't get your email.

Me: Yes you did. And you opened and read it twice.

Them: What? How do you know this.

Me: This isn't my first rodeo, when I need to send something important I track it. In your case an invoice.

Them: What? That's invasion of privacy or something.

Me: No, it's taking advantage of technology to know when someone opens the email I send them.

Them: So I read it, so what.

Me: So now you admit you lied.

Them: Well, you're sending trackable email, that's kind of weird.

Me: Again, available technology.

Them: I don't know if I can trust you.

Me: Says the guy who just lied to me.

Them: Yeah, but you're tracking email and knowing when we open and read it. That's just wrong.

Me: Would you like to know how to track your own email?

Them: Heck yeah.

Me: Wow a hypocrite too.

Them: You're a jerk.

Me: So is that a YES or NO to the email I sent you?

Them: YES, I will get a payment to you .

Me: Thank you.

Them: {mumbles}

{Got payment 5 minutes later}

Want to know what program I use to track emails?

Send an email to: info@anspachmedia.com

with the subject line: ***Tracking Emails***

Replying To Unsolicited Email

Greetings I hope this email finds you well.

Me: Actually no, your email was the cause of my injury which required 3 excruciating nights at St John's Hospital.

Them: That's fantastic. Can we share with you our fabulous services?

Me: Unless your services include physical therapy and plenty of Netflix watching I don't think you can help me.

Them: We can have one of our representatives reach out and explain our system and how it works, would that be acceptable?

Me: Acceptable? No, not at all.

Them: In addition to our previous email I would like to share with you our Trial Project as well as win your faith with our best services and initiate our relations to go a long way.

Me: Sounds like a bunch of nonsense, I'm in.

Them: And for this project we will not charge you anything if you do not like the work done from my side without asking anything.

Me: No idea where you learned grammar, but I like it.

Them: More info this I would like to share you that we work on Fixed Cost and Hourly basis and per your or project requirements.

Me: Go on.

Them: Further request you to share your best available time and contact number or Skype ID to discuss the possibilities of working together.

Me: Sounds like endless wonder, can't wait.

Them: Feel free to advise me your views or let me know to remove your mail ID from my list.

Me: My views? You want me to advise you on my views? What kind of freak are you. I'm out. Remove me from your list.

Them: We believe in quick and up-front communication with this we have achieved good satisfaction ratio with our on-going client's in terms of producing quality work with efficiency and within defined timelines.

Me: Oh, kill me now.

Note: Its best just to delete these emails instead of engaging with them. But where's the fun in that?

I Don't Want To Unsubscribe

"Rob I get an email from you every single day."

Me: And?

Well it's a lot.

Me: Well you can unsubscribe if it's too much.

No, I don't want to unsubscribe.

Me: Okay what's the problem then?

Well I just think every day is too much.

Me: Well then, how about you only read them on days you want to read them.

Well if you send them to me I will read them.

Me: I really don't understand what you want then.

Well, could you not send them to me every day?

Me: Which days do you not want to read them?

I don't know.

Me: Well I don't know either. So, again I will continue to send them and you only read them on days you feel like reading them. Or you can unsubscribe.

NOTE: Yes, I Email My Subscribers Every Day!

My goal is to deliver content that is entertaining, educational and engaging every single day. That content, whatever it may be, is designed to give you an insight and understanding in how YOU can create a business that reflects YOU unto the customer.

If you would like to subscribe (and yes I make it easy to unsubscribe) go to my website right now and fill in your information. You'll learn stuff.

Rob Anspach

Chapter 6

The Closer

"Although I think his rap name is C-Loser."

LinkedIn Is Not For This Closer

Another so-called "Closer" ends his short lived LinkedIn friendship with me. Well, I'll give him credit he did hang in there for a few days.

Them: (Aug 11) Pleasure to e-meet. I came across your profile via mutual connections; thought I would reach out to connect virtually. Please don't hesitate to reach out if you have any questions RE: how we can scale your business by leveraging our closing team.

Them: (Aug 12) I know we just connected, but I wanted to reach out. It looks like you are in a similar field to many of my clients. I have been leading sales teams for some time and I've noticed that many of our clients are excellent at what they do, but often struggle or find it difficult to capitalize on the leads they've worked so hard to cultivate... Alone. This is where my company steps in to retain and enroll your new customers from these leads. Having a talent and passion for sales has allowed me to create a bigger, wider impact through my clients as we scale their businesses. I'd love to learn more about who you serve and in what capacity. And of course, once I have a better understanding of what you do, I would be more than happy to send any referrals your way. Cheers P.S. If you prefer, we can set up a call. Use my schedule link

Me: (Aug 12) I take it you actually didn't read my profile because had you...you would know exactly what I do.

Them: (Aug 13) I was under the impression you ran a business in the marketing world, in which you sold your services in various packages to clients that need your expertise. If this isn't the case then I apologize.

Me: (Aug 13) And I need your services why?

Two days later I was unfriended.

Note: I cringe every time I accept a new LinkedIn friend request as 90% of them will send me some spammy sales pitch five seconds after acceptance. And I find the majority of those who list "Closer" in their profile have all gone to the same idiot school of blasting pitches out to everyone without understanding who they are or what their needs are. Grr.

A Recent Facebook Chat

Rob, what do you do when you have a free day that you aren't helping clients?

Me: I work on my marketing.

Them: Really?

Me: Yup, I try to always keep my marketing planned out and scheduled at least 60 days ahead.

Them: Wow.

Me: Yup, for the last week in between helping clients, I wrote 15 more blogs for my website and 90 emails for my daily subscriber email newsletter.

Them: Amazing.

Me: Well, thank you...but, it's something I do every single day for my clients so why shouldn't my marketing be planned ahead too.

Them: But how do you do it all...are you the King of Content Creation?

Me: I like that...I suppose I am.

Can You Optimize My Website

Hey Rob, can you optimize my website?

Was the chat message I received through Facebook.

Me: Most likely.

Them: I thought you were the master at SEO, why do you say most likely?

Me: I find that some sites, those designed to be more cut and paste for the DIY'er tend not to be SEO friendly even if they advertise they are.

Them: So you can't optimize them.

Me: I can, but my fee to do so tends to be more than the cost they shelled out for that site initially.

Them: Oh.

Me: And those sites tend to take longer to rank in the search engines even when properly optimized

Them: Ah.

Me: Yup, that's why I say most likely.

Them: Okay.

Me: So do you have a site you want me to look at?

Them: Hmm, no.

Me: You have one of those cut and paste sites don't you?

Them: Yes.

Me: It's time to upgrade then...my team can help build you a new site, that's optimized, mobile friendly and starts to rank on the search engines almost immediately.

Them: Can't right now no budget for a new website, could you recommend someone cheap that could help us with SEO.

Me: Do you want someone good or cheap? Because you already went down the road with a cheap website and see where that got you.

The person unfriended and blocked me.

Note: Proper website optimization isn't cheap. However, if you have WIX, Square Space or a website that is not built using WordPress, the fee for us to help you will most likely far exceed what you paid to have the site built.

Chapter 7

Getting Reported

"And, it was so much fun too!"

I'm Not The IT Department... or Am I?

7:04am Monday - my cell phone rings

Me: This is Rob.

Them: Is this the I.T. department?
{me not wanting to disappoint them}

Me: Sure is, how can I help?

Them: My computer stopped working?

Me: Is it turned on?

Them: {short pause} What kind of dumb question is that?

Me: There is no such thing as dumb questions, just dumb people asking questions. So is it turned on?

Them: {short pause} No.

Me: Can you turn it on?

Them: {longer pause} Okay, it's on now.

Me: Is it working?

Them: Hmm, err, yeah.

Me: Now don't you feel silly?

Them: You're an ass, I'm reporting you to Human Resources.

Me: Oh no, not Human Resources, say it isn't so.

Them: Yes, you're arrogant and obnoxious.

Me: And?

Them: IT Support is supposed to be nice and friendly and not condescending.

Me: Well, had you actually called the real IT department maybe they would be, but you called me...

Them: {cutting me off before I could finish what I was going to say, which was probably good because it wasn't nice} What? What do you mean it's not the real IT Department?

Me: {thinking gawd how long can I keep this moron on the phone} Well, let me tell you a story of a guy who dialed the wrong number only to have another guy answer that call who really only wanted to waste his time. Oh, you'll love this story. It's got computers, smart ass comments and a fantastic surprise ending.

Them: F-You

Me: Is that anyway to say thanks for getting your computer to work?

<they hung up>

5 minutes later...my phone rings

Me: This is Rob.

Them: This is Human Resources, we'll need you to come down and explain your actions from your support call a few minutes ago.

Me: Come down? I don't even know where you're located.

Them: {short pause} We're on the 3rd floor.

Me: Oh, yes that explains so much.

Them: Excuse me?

Me: You say you're on the 3rd floor, the 3rd floor of what building, where?

Them: Huh, where are you?

Me: I'm here.

Them: Yes, where's here?

Me: That's really the wrong question. The question isn't where I am, it's really who I am?

Them: Who are you?

Me: Well, I'm not an IT guy and I don't work for your company, but have I got a story for you...

Them: {cutting me off} What do you mean you're not an IT guy and you don't work at this company?

Me: Well, I tell you what, instead of me coming down to see you, come on up to the IT department and we can have a discussion. I'll be the guy laughing my ass off.

<they hung up>

I really hope there is no ROB in their IT department - ooh, he's gonna get fired.

Note: If you're going to call me, make sure it's actually me you're looking for, otherwise you might just become a story in my next book.

Rules, What Rules?

Rob, you can't say that to a customer. You can't treat them like that. And the customer is always right.

Me: Says who?

Well, all the customer service gurus out there.

Me: Pfft!

Are you saying you don't agree or they are wrong?

Me: I've been an entrepreneur for 25 plus years and I've found being me (my sarcastic self) makes me more money than trying to be a disciple of the customer service rules and regulations.

But Rob you're wrong.

Me: Am I really?

Yes I think so.

Me: Nope, I run my business how I see fit, taking on clients who match my personality and I don't have to grovel to the whims of "I'm the customer and I'm right" demands.

Wow, and you still have customers.

Me: Yup.

I would never hire you.

Me: Says the guy who is already my client paying me a fortune to help him.

Oh right.

Me: See my system works.

Note: Those who have an awesome business have learned to embrace their authenticity. So if you truly want to be authentic then you need to allow your personality to shine. You don't have to please everyone, just the ones that matter.

Other People Named "Rob Anspach"

Hey Rob, you should read "*Lessons From The Dojo*" it's written by a guy with your name.

Me: Yes, I wrote it... in 2015.

Them: No way.

Me: Yes way.

Them: Really.

Me: Yup.

Them: Wow.

Me: Why wow?

Them: Just didn't put two and two together I guess.

Me: So you know of other people named "Rob Anspach"

Them: No just you.

Me: And you didn't think I wrote it.

Them: It just didn't occur to me.

Me: Well I've authored, coauthored or produced over 2 dozen books in 6 years.

Them: Wow.

Me: Yup, wow.

Them: How did you get started?

Me: Just started writing.

Them: Oh.

Me: Were you expecting something more dramatic, magical or inspiring.

Them: A bit.

Me: Nope, just start writing.

Note: The very first lesson in my book "Lessons From The Dojo" is *Overnight Success Begins By Mastering The Basics*. And it's those basics that enable you, when improved upon, to become better every day to the point that others deem you an overnight success.

Chapter 8

Just Pay Me

"Businesses would be more profitable if they just remembered those three words."

Why I Don't Accept Payments For One-Time Services

Hey Rob, can I make payments?

Me: The service you selected is a one-time, non-monthly contract so the amount will need to be paid in full.

Them: But we would like to make payments.

Me: Pay the whole amount using a credit card and you can make payments to the credit card company.

Them: We don't use credit cards.

Me: And I don't make payment arrangements for a one off service.

Them: Why not? Other's do.

Me: You are free to go use any of the so-called others you speak of.

Them: Well we want to use your services.

Me: Then stop arguing about my payment terms and pay the amount in question.

Them: But we want...

Me: Yes, I heard what you want and if you want my service then you need to comply with my terms.

Them: I'm the customer and the customer is always right .

Me: Except when they are wrong and can't understand that it's my business and my rules, if you want to play my game you need to follow my rules.

Them: Well we need payments.

Me: This is becoming a circular conversation, and frankly I'm not interested in going round and round anymore.

Them: What's that supposed to mean?

Me: It means call someone else to have your small project done.

Them: Who?

Me: I don't really care as long as it's not me.

Them: What's the reason?

Me: I think we've already established that reason, have you not been paying attention the last few minutes?

Them: Yes.

Me: Okay final time, I will not accept payments on a one-time, non-monthly contract. You pay upfront and we provide service. No payment, no work. Got it.

Them: Not really.

Me: I'm not sure where the disconnect is so I'm going to help you out...

{ I hung up }

{15 minutes later receive an email asking if they can pay with a credit card}

Note: Some of you might be shaking your head thinking, "*wow must be nice to turn away money*". But, it's not a case of turning money away, it's a case of preventing my company from being ripped off. When you offer payments on one-time services you are inviting a client to basically take advantage of you, delay payment or deny payment when then didn't get the results they think they should have. Making customers comply with your payment policies eliminates problems caused by non-payments.

Do You Work For Free

I highly doubt it.

Okay, then why do you assume I will?

{I had to fire a client today. Mind you it wasn't a big client. But they expected since we hosted their website on our servers that we would give them free service above and beyond what we offer on our hosting package. So I sent them an invoice for our expected time to cover what they wanted done.}

They flipped out. They said it was outrageous. And that the invoice was too much for the time needed to perform such duties.

My reply..."how so?"

Them: Well that's not what others charge.

Me: So you expect me to charge what others charge?

Them: Yes I do.

Me: So you do expect to pay something.

Them: No you should give it to me for free since I pay for hosting.

Me: So because you pay for one service you expect a completely different service to be done by my team at no charge.

Them: Yes or at a reduced price.

Me: So what is it, you want me to work for free or at a reduced rate?

Them: Preferably for FREE.

Me: How many clients do you work for FREE?

Them: None.

Me: Then why do you expect me to do it?

Them: Because it should only take you a few minutes and you are charging me too much for it.

Me: Actually, I'm not charging you enough.

Them: What?

Me: That is my reduced rate for those that host with us. But hosting and the service you needed done are two separate things.

Them: That's ridiculous.

Me: What's ridiculous is your attitude. How about you find another hosting service.

Them: I still have 4 months left.

Me: Do you?

Them: I think so.

Me: Then pay my invoice.

Them: No.

Me: Then your hosting is terminated.

Them: But you said it's two separate things.

Me: Apparently not, according to you.

Them: This sucks.

Me: What sucks is when clients think I work for FREE then get themselves fired for undervaluing what I do for them.

Note: Customers who expect you to work for FREE should be fired immediately. As they have no respect for the value that your provide to them.

Choosing Between A Great Team Or A Cheap Service

Hey Rob, we would really like your team to rebuild our website.

Me: Great!

Them: But we got a super cheap price from another company.

Me: Okay then go with them.

Them: But we want your team.

Me: So do you want cheap or do you want me and my team?

Them: Well can you lower your price?

Me: No!

Them: Well I would like to share their price with you and what they are offering.

{price is 60% less and missing half of what we included}

Me: Their price and service doesn't even compare with what we are offering.

Them: But we need a lower price.

Me: Then go with the other company.

Them: But we would like your team.

Me: This is a circular conversation.

Them: A what?

Me: We are going round and round and you're not hearing what I'm saying.

Them: Yes I am, we just need a lower price.

Me: Think of my price as the more value centric price when you factor in all the extra stuff we are giving you that the other company isn't.

Them: Why didn't you say that before?

{Me totally ignoring his question}

Me: Let me know if you need anything else.

Them: Will get back to you in an hour.

{15 minutes later}

Them: Hey Rob, my team still wants a lower price.

Me: We had this conversation before, my answer hasn't changed.

Them: But...

Me: Here I'll make it easy for you... hire the other company. In fact, give me their number and I'll accept their deal on your behalf.

Them: What?

Me: Look if you want my team then my price is the price - if you want a lower price you need to go somewhere else.

{I hung up}

*Received email 20 minutes later asking for a lower price.

Note: The moment you lower your price to try to be a hero to someone who can't afford you, is the moment you become the victim. You will spend too much time, energy and heartache trying to help them and it'll bite you in the end. Stick to your price. And if means turning work away, then do it.

Chapter 9

X Plus $10,000

"It's a simple formula that eliminates so many hassles."

Firing Clients Before They Even Begin

Don't you just love when someone says, "I was expecting a detailed proposal!" After you just sent them a full page quote that explained everything you are doing for them. And then you scratch your head thinking, WTF! So you reach out to them and ask them why they were expecting such a thing. And they respond, "well if I'm going to spend X, then you should tell me exactly what I'm getting."

Me: Hmm, I did tell you exactly what you were getting.

Them: But not in detail.

Me: So basically you want me to fluff up the proposal to make you feel all warm and fuzzy inside.

Them: Yes.

Me: Fine, that'll be an extra $10,000, how would you like to pay?

Them: What?

Me: Look, I gave you a quote that spelled out what you were getting, that wasn't good enough for you. So now you want me to enhance my proposal and fill it with rainbows and unicorns just so you feel I'm the service for you. Well, for me to do that will cost you an extra

$10,000. So do you want to pay X or X plus $10,000 your choice.

Them: Well I want a detailed proposal.

Me: Okay then it's X plus $10,000 then.

Them: No I don't want to pay $10,000 extra.

Me: Fine, then it's just X

Them: No.

Me: Look you either choose X or X plus $10,000

Them: Well I want X but in more detail.

Me: So X plus $10,000

Them: But I don't want to pay an extra $10,000.

Me: And I don't want to spend extra time fluffing up a proposal I already gave you.

Them: Well how about I go somewhere else then?

Me: Please do.

Them: But I really want you to help me.

Me: Too late.

Them: What?

Me: You already opened up the door, step through it now.

Them: Huh?

Me: If you are going somewhere else, go.

Them: Mm, can we start over?

Me: Sure pay X in the next 24 hours and we can begin.

Them: Can you get me a detailed proposal?

Me: You're fired!

Them: But I haven't even paid you yet.

Me: Don't bother.

Them: So I can't hire you?

Me: Not for X and not for X plus $10,000...you're just not worth the hassle. Buh-bye!

Note: Too much detail in your proposals will give the client a way to shop you and / or do the job themselves. Make your proposals in such a way as to not give every detail away.

No Quote For You!

Hey Rob, can you give me a quote?

Me: It depends.

Them: What do you mean it depends? Either you can or you can't.

Me: Do you need the service now or later?

Them: Why?

Me: Well if I quote you a price now then that price is valid for the next 25 days. But if you want a quote for work that you want in the next 30, 60, 90 or 180 days or more, than the price has to be reflective of future costs.

Them: That's not how your competitors work.

Me: Not sure who you are referring to, but I have no competitors.

Them: Sure you do.

Me: I get the feeling you really don't want a quote you just want to argue.

Them: I have quotes from several others who claim to do what you do...

Me: Then why do you need a quote from me?

Them: Well, you've been highly recommended and we wanted to see how you compare.

Me: I don't compare...like I said I have no competitors.

Them: Sure you do.

Me: Please hire one of those so-called competitors then, I'm not interested.

Them: What? We could have given you lots of money.

Me: The key phrase there is "could have". I doubt the money would be worth the hassle.

{caller hung up}

{Five minutes later received an email asking for a quote}

Note: Learn to say NO to customers that just don't fit.

And It Was Going So Well Until...

Hey Rob, can I be honest with you?

Me: So you've been lying to me up to this point?

Them: What?

Me: You wanted to know if you could be honest with me and I pointed out that you must have been lying prior to asking.

Them: Ugh, you're impossible.

Me: Well, at least I'm not a liar.

FYI: If you are one to say, "can I be honest with you", you might want to stop saying that. Otherwise you might just have someone call you a liar.

Chapter 10

Chief Instigator

"What else would you expect from me?"

Dealing With Obnoxious Follow-Ups

Filled out a form online on Saturday.

Sunday I received a text, phone call, voicemail and email from them asking if I have questions about their service.

I reply to their text..."It's Sunday, call back Monday."

So then they call me...

Me: Hello.

Them: Is this Rob?

Me: Who's this?

Them: {telling me the name of the service}

Me: It's Sunday, can you call back on Monday?

Them: You answered the phone, evidently you are working.

Me: No I'm not.
{I hung up}

They emailed me to say how rude I was.

Told them to remove me from their list.

To which they reply... "gladly".

Yet, they text me a survey to see how well I enjoyed their service.

FAIL, FAIL and FAIL.

To which prompts another idiot from their service to call, text, email and leave a voicemail.

OMG.

Note: Follow ups should not be intrusive and should stop immediately when a person expresses their concern, yet, the majority of those performing the follow ups only persist in annoying the customer.

I'm Your Huckleberry

Well that's what I thought he said when I answered the phone.

Me: You're my what? Huckleberry?

Them: No, this is Cole from Huckleberry.

Me: Okay and?

Them: I see you started to fill out a form on our website but didn't complete it.

Me: Hmm, I don't recall. But if I didn't finish I was either (1) not impressed with the site (2) it asked for way too much information (3) I was bored with it or (4) decided it wasn't worth my time.

Them: Well I'd be glad to capture that information from you right now and we can finish the form together.

Me: And how long will that take?

Them: About 5 minutes or so.

Me: So basically double the time it would take me on your site.

Them: Yes, but I can answer your questions while I have you on the phone.

Me: Let's review the reasons I didn't finish filling out your form to begin with.

Them: Can I get your full company name and address.

Me: I'd rather not.

Them: What is your title in the company.

Me: Chief Instigator

Them: Sir if you're not going to take this serious I don't think we can help you.

Me: If I was serious I would have finished filling out your form, but I didn't. And then you called and I had to explain the reasons why I didn't fill out the form. But you want me to be serious with you so you can help me, when I really don't need your service.

Them: Apparently today is not a good day for you, I'll call back another time.

Me: And you won't be my Huckleberry then either.

FYI: Getting a phone call immediately after deciding not to fill in a form is creepy as heck. Don't do it. Sending an email or even a text message is less intrusive and produces a better response rate.

Chapter 11

Staying Loyal

"Being rewarded for loyalty never felt so exhausting."

We Will Annoy You To Keep You Safe

Grr... so I go online and make a huge payment to one of my Credit Cards.

Then I get an email asking me if I just made the payment for X amount. Then 30 minutes later I get a phone call asking me if indeed I made that payment. I say this is why I pay online so I can save time and not have to deal with emails and phone calls.

Credit Card Co Rep: Sir these are new policies that we implemented to keep you safe?

Me: Safe from whom...are there people out there who pay other people's credit card balances?

Credit Card Co Rep: Well Sir, these are extra steps we take to keep you safe?

Me: Well, I don't need an email or a phone call asking me to reconfirm my payment. That just wastes my time.

Credit Card Co Rep: Unfortunately Sir, based on the amount of your payment you will get an email and phone call from us.

Me: Okay what is the threshold of payment to not trigger an email and phone call?

Credit Card Co Rep: XXX (which incidentally is $1 less than I paid)

Me: Seriously?

Credit Card Co Rep: Yes Sir.

Me: So to not trigger your dumb email or nuisance call I need to lower my payment or make two payments?

Credit Card Co Rep: That's partially correct Sir...you can lower your payment under the threshold but you can't make 2 payments within a 24 hour period nor can you have more than 1 payment pre-scheduled at a time.

Me: So now I need to make multiple payments and waste more time, or make one large payment and deal with your email and phone call?

Credit Card Co Rep: That is correct Sir?

Me: How about I change my contact email and phone number so you can't bug me?

Credit Card Co Rep: Sir, you may do that, but if we don't get a confirmation from you, your payment won't be processed and you will be charged a late fee.

Me: This seems like a no win situation.

Credit Card Co Rep: For you yes, for us no.

Me: Well, I'll tell you what...cancel my card and close my account.

Credit Card Co Rep: Sir, if I make sure we don't call you will you still stay a loyal customer?

Me: I don't know...not feeling it.

Credit Card Co Rep: How about a lower interest rate?

Me: And?

Credit Card Co Rep: We can increase your credit limit.

Me: And?

Credit Card Co Rep: You can skip two payments in a 12 month period without interest or penalty.

Me: Deal.

{After I hung up, I received an email and another phone call}

Note: Policies and protocols that frustrate customers should be simplified. Customer service reps need to be empowered to help customers not irritate them further.

Your Reason Is Invalid

Apparently my AAA card expired. So I called them. OMG.

Sir, why did you let your membership expire?

Me: Hmm, do I have to have a reason?

Well Sir, if you would like us to reactivate your old number we need a valid reason why you forgot to renew.

Me: Seriously, can't you just renew the card?

No Sir, we need a valid reason.

Me: How about I just get a brand new membership and not give you a reason at all?

Sir, just give me a reason and we can activate your card.

Me: I forgot.

Sir, you forgot what?

Me: Why the hell did I even bother to call you?

Sir, you called to renew your membership.

Me: There you go.

Sir, there I go what?

Me: Use that as my reason.

Sir, what reason?

Me: Never mind…I think waterboarding myself would be more pleasant than staying on this call.

Have fun with that Sir.

<they hung up>

FYI: Having a "no questions asked policy" makes it easier for clients to want to renew.

I Can't Assist You

Sir, unfortunately you called the wrong department, I can't assist you.

You need to call (gives 10 digit number)

Me: That's the number I called.

Sir did you press option 6, then 1, then 2.

Me: Well I did press 6 then 1 but honestly I have no idea after that.

Sir, I can transfer you.

Me: Thank you.

{music plays in background while the person transfers me}

Hi Sir how can I help you?

Me: Hmm, didn't I just speak to you.

Sir? No Sir, I don't believe so.

Me: Your name is Shaniqua right?

Well that is my name.

Me: So you did just take my call, place me on hold then transfer the call back to yourself.

No Sir, you must be mistaken.

Me: Or your company only hires people with your name and voice to answer all the calls.

{she hung up on me}

Note: If you are the one answering calls and you make a mistake own up to it, apologize to the customer then transfer them to the right department.

Why The Reference Number

Sir thank you for calling, here's your reference number if you need to call back, just refer to that number and the person taking your call will be up to speed.

Then you call back, give them the reference number and then spend the next ½ hour explaining everything to the person taking the call.

Me: Can't you just read the notes.

Them: Sir, there is no notes.

Me: Okay then what is the point in giving me a reference number?

Them: Sir, all calls are supposed to be given a reference number.

Me: So are you going to give me a reference number before this call is over.

Them: Yes.

Me: And if I call back will I need to give the next person all my information again.

Them: Yes.

Me: Then why do you even give reference numbers out.

Them: Because it helps makes the customer happy.

Me: You know what actually makes us happy, is you taking copious notes so we don't have to repeat ourselves multiple times.

Them: Sir that's not how it works.

Me: Yes it is! That's actually how it's supposed to work.

Note: Don't be that company above. If a customer calls your help line and your representative gives out a reference number they'd better have had taken detailed notes. When customers have problems they want a company that at least attempts to care.

Argumentative Telephone Tech

Voicemail not displaying on my wife's iPhone.

I call ATT to get an answer. The rep asked for my name, mobile number, address and last 4 digits of my credit card.

Then the rep asks for my PIN number. So I tell him.

He says that PIN is incorrect. I say that PIN is correct. No Sir, it's now an 8 digit PIN.

Me: Since when.

ATT: Since you last changed it

Me: And that was?

ATT: Unknown Sir, would you like to reset it?

Me: Can we skip the reset and just fix my wife's phone?

ATT: Sir we need the PIN first.

Me: Look it was a 4 digit PIN, then a 6 digit PIN, now you say it's 8 digits...and the next time I call it will be 12 digits then 20 digits and before long a 30 digit alpha numeric code.

ATT: Sir you are being ridiculous, let's just reset the PIN.

Me: Just fix the phone.

ATT: Sir I can't do anything without the PIN.

Me: Well apparently you can argue without a PIN.

<He hung up>

FYI: If you already have all my information don't make me jump through hoops to prove who I am.

Mister Impatient

Hey, Rob I called you twice today.

Me: Did you leave a message?

Them: No.

Me: Then it wasn't important.

Them: Yes, it was.

Me: If it was you'd have left a message.

Them: I emailed you too.

Me: Emailed it to where?

Them: When you didn't respond I called again.

Me: And yet you didn't leave a message.

Them: Well, now I have you here on Facebook chat.

Me: Yup, probably should have started with that first.

Them: Why didn't you answer the phone.

Me: Because I'm busy and these interruptions cost me time.

Them: Do you want to call me back?

Me: Dude, I don't even know what you want.

Them: I need help.

Me: I get that...what type of help? And if you say "your help" I'm blocking your ass.

Them: Forget it, you're impossible.

Me: No, I'm focused and you're wasting my time.

Them: Well pick up the phone next time and we won't have these dumb chats.

Me: Oh yes it's my fault, I forgot who I was dealing with.

Them: What's that supposed to mean.

Me: Look Mr. Impatient, if you leave a message next time I will respond when I have time, not when you believe I should respond.

Them: That's a dumb rule.

Me: Take or leave it, my rules, my game.

Them: When can we chat.

Me: We are chatting.

Them: On the phone.

Me: OMG – we are chatting here now, spill it, what's on your mind?

Them: I need to talk to you.

Me: And I need to be waterboarded.

Them: Why?

Me: Because it would be more pleasant than this chat.

<they immediately blocked me>

Note: Technology is wonderful isn't it? Yet, when placed in the wrong hands it becomes a weapon of irritation. And irritating someone just doesn't make them want to help you.

Chapter 12

Trust Us

"Just another term for bend over and take it."

You Want To Send Me A What?

Hey Rob, can we send you our dynamic new DVD to watch?

Me: Seriously? Can't you just email me a link to watch it?

Caller: No, our policy is to mail you a DVD.

Me: I'll pass then.

Caller: It's a fantastic presentation, you'll enjoy it.

Me: Well, if you send me a link I can enjoy it sooner, like right now.

Caller: It will only take 2-3 weeks to get to you, I'm sure it'll be worth the wait.

Me: I could be dead in 2-3 weeks.

Caller: Well, in the case you're still alive you have something to look forward to.

Me: I could be watching your presentation right now while you answered my questions.

Caller: So no DVD then?

Me: What do you think?
(The caller hung up)

Demonstration Fail

Hi Rob, we would like to set up a demonstration of our services with you.

Me: Why?

Them: We believe we can help you automate your social media, email and CRM systems.

Me: How'd you hear about me?

Them: We have people that scroll the internet.

Me: What's your website?

{shares website with me, probably shouldn't have as I basically ripped the SEO apart.

Them: The site is still being built out.

Me: Then why share it?

Them: You asked.

Me: $49.95 for your middle package seems on par with what other systems like yours are doing, but the $3000 fee to set up the account is ridiculous.

Them: The rep doing the demo has the power to waive that fee if he/she chooses.

Me: Why would they if they are working on commission?

Them: Good question, I'll get back to you on that.

{me jumping on their Facebook page}

Me: So I'm on your Facebook page and I see you don't post every day. In fact your last post was 5 days ago and the one before that was 3 days prior and it looks like you post on average every 3-4 days.

Them: Yes, we are working on that.

Me: Yet, you want me to say YES to buying into your system that seems incomplete and ill-prepared to post for me.

Them: Sir, that's why we would like to schedule a demonstration.

Me: I teach my clients to post to their social media pages consistently. At least once a day. This helps them connect to their audience and build trust.

Them: Trust us, we know what we are doing, and...

{click, me hanging up}

Backup Recovery Hosting Hassles

Sir, your website package has no backup recovery function.

{me on the phone with tech support trying to get a client's website to roll back to a time before it was updated by a non-supporting theme which broke the site}

Me: Are you kidding me? What kind of whack-a-do operation you got going over there? This is precisely why we implemented our own hosting platform for our clients so they always had the ability to recover their site when needed.

Them: Sir, I assure we will make this right for you and your client. And this one time restore we will do at no charge to your client.

Me: I hope so.

Them: What date were you looking to roll back the site to? {gives three options}

Me: The middle date.

Them: Okay, we can do that. May I suggest adding "backup recovery" to your clients account.

Me: What? That should be something you include. We include it free to our clients.

Them: No Sir, it's an extra $14.99 a year.

Me: Seriously, that's $1.25 a month – just add it to their package and call it a value added service.

Them: Sir, makes sense, but we can't.

Me: When can I tell my client to expect his website to be recovered?

Them: 24 hours.

Me: Okay, expect a call if it's not restored.

{25 hours later, me on the phone with them again}

Them: Hi Sir, yes we have a record of you calling, but the support ticket is blank.

Me: So me being on the phone yesterday was what...a test run?

Them: Sir, you wanted the website removed correct?

Me: So help me if you idiots remove the site...you were supposed to do a backup recovery to the date specified.

Them: Sir that date is not available.

Me: WTF!

Them: It might have been when you called, but it's 24 hours later so it's no longer available – will the next dated file work.

Me: Yes, okay fix it.

Them: Sir we have escalated this the 2nd level support team and they will take care of this in 24-48 hours.

Me: Not acceptable. You already wasted 24 hours.

Them: Okay, Sir we will fast track it.

Me: Email me the progress.

{gets my email address to keep me in the loop on recovery process}

{20 minutes I receive an email}

Them (via email): We have started the process of recovery, can you ask your client to approve the cost of $100 for recovery.

Me: No, I will not ask my client, your technician agreed to have it done for FREE.

Them: Oh, okay.

{5 minutes later}

Them: Sir please check site now, should be recovered.

NOTE: I deal with this shit all the time, hosting companies trying to nickel and dime the client for every little thing. WE don't do that. Our hosting package is all inclusive and comes with continuous backup and recovery, security protocols to ward against hackers and intrusion and 24/7 tech support to give you peace of mind.

Chapter 13

The F-You Awards

There's a special place in HELL for these bastards…

"…if only they would stay there!"

The Top Level I F-You Award Goes To...

This one goes to Google for completely and utterly jacking my blood pressure to the point I wanted to reach into the phone and strangle the call center technician.

My client's Google My Business (GMB) website link was being diverted to a Viagra site and it was only from the tabs on GMB profile, nowhere else.

After dealing with the first patronizing technician who kept trying to email me (misspelling the email twice) and then blaming me for not receiving said email. Then after sharing the screen and proving to her that my clients GMB listing was being redirected she still wanted to blame my clients website. It's not a website problem I would argue, stating that no other place on the whole internet does it redirect, except for GMB.

Then after requesting a second technician help me (Google's call center is not in the USA) I was patronized once again. Forced to repeat everything I said to the first technician and this so-called I didn't really want to listen to what I was saying. Finally I said, "I'm done with you, put someone else on the phone."

Sir there is no one else, I am the Top Level rep here.

Me: Well, then transfer me to somewhere else as you have no clue what you are doing.

Sir, I assure you the error is on your clients website and not from Google.

Me: I have already explained the problems more than once, I shared my screen and showed you the problems, and I showed you that the error is coming from GMB

Sir, our system is so integrated that the listing on Google should be showing the same information on the GMB listing.

Me: Were you not paying attention to the screen share or the fact your system is not working.

Sir I assure you it's your clients website that is in error.

Me: Put someone else on the phone.

Sir, there is no one above me.

Me: Fine put the janitor on the phone, at least he will listen.

Sir he quit.

Me: Yeah maybe you should too.

I hung up.

The Customer Service F-You Award Goes To

On a quest for soccer cleats for my youngest son.

We ended up stopping at Wendy's for a bite to eat.

Had we found those cleats I think I would have kicked all the employees at Wendy's in their backside.

We waited 20 minutes for our order. And the 100 choices soda dispenser was down to about 4 weird flavors that nobody in their right mind would ever drink.

Customers would walk in and after a few minutes in line would leave.

One customer ordered then after waiting 10 minutes demanded their money back.

The manager was in the back chatting away with the 2 or 3 cook staff and a young gal who never dealt with irate customers before was left to tend the register.

And that young gal instead of apologizing to customers (which she probably wasn't trained to do) copped an attitude and just made customers madder.

It took us 30 minutes to receive our "fast" food.

The Communication F-You Award Goes To

Forty-five days later... I receive a response to a question I emailed Allegiant Airlines.

Look I wasn't expecting them to drop everything and answer my email.

I figured maybe at best 2-3 days I would get a response.

I was planning a trip 6 months out although I didn't tell them that. I just wanted clarification on something they had shared on their website.

After a week of no response I actually booked my trip with another air carrier.

Another carrier who responded immediately to my email and made me feel welcome.

But 45 days later and I receive...
"Thank you for contacting Allegiant. You have reached the Customer Relations Department. I apologize for the delayed response. We are experiencing a high demand in emails, and we are trying our best to respond as quickly as possible. I am very sorry that you are getting this email late."

The Medical Billing F-You Award Goes To

A big "F-You" goes to Penn Medicine Health billing department.

They've been emailing me an invoice that includes a link to their payment processor that I can't open because they don't include any corresponding information with it.

When I call to get clarification they said sorry you are not on the account.

And I reply...then stop emailing me then.

On Saturday they mailed me a **FINAL INVOICE**.

So I call again and told them to stop emailing me and send me a real printed invoice.

Them: Sorry Sir, you are not on the account and if you wish to be off of paperless billing then you will need to go to our online system and change how communication is sent. And you should be added as a responsible party.

Me: I thought I was a responsible party. How can I pay this invoice right now?

Them: Sir, as I explained you will need to go online to pay the bill.

Me: So you put me on paperless billing with no ability to pay the bill, send me a Final Notice to call you to take care of said payment yet make me go back online to pay the bill. Do you really want paid?

Them: Sir, please follow the instructions.

Me: Nah, I'm done. Send it to collections I will probably have a better chance paying them.

The Online Chat F-You Award Goes To

On chat with Comcast...

{Gave my name & account information, then explained what was happening to my service.}

Comcast: Please let me know what can I do to help.

Me: How the hell should I know...isn't that your job?

Comcast: Sir?

Me: You should be trained to help me. If I knew how to be helped in this situation I would be doing your job.

{they disconnected me from chat – guess I was supposed to help myself}

The Check Out F-You Award Goes To

Had to go to Kmart to find something...UGH!

One register open...I'm 5 deep in line wondering what the hell is taking these morons so long to get the heck out of the store.

Okay my turn...

Sir do you have a Kmart rewards card?

Me: Just ring me up, I'm in a hurry.

Cashier: But it will only take a second.

Me: No just ring the purchase up please.

Cashier: Please look at the card terminal and answer the questions...
{Do you want to donate to St Jude's Hospital}

Me: I rather not answer any questions, because I just want to get out the door.

Cashier: Please just answer the card terminal question.

Me: For the love of Pete...just ring the damn purchase up.

{Me pressing NO I don't want to give}

Cashier: Now answer the next question.
{now there are 5 people in back of me, staring at me and wondering why the asshole is taking so long to buy his shit}

Me: WTF

{Do you want your receipt printed, emailed or both}

Me: Can I just have the receipt.

Cashier: Sir you have to press the button saying your choice.

Me: Did I die? Is this hell?

Cashier: Thank you Sir, here's your receipt. Come again soon.

{Next customer already had the sad look of defeat on her face as she stepped up to start the process of paying for her stuff.)

Chapter 14

Stupid Is As Stupid Does

"And sadly, stupid does seem to work everywhere."

A Priest, A Rabbi & The President

Hello, thank you for calling XYZ Co.

Can I get your name.
{so I give them my name}

Sir, that name is not on file.

Me: Of course it isn't, the account is in my business name.

Okay we will look up the account based on the number you are calling on.

Me: Why?

Sir, hang on please while I look up your account.

Me: Grr.

Sir, that number doesn't match our files.

Me: Yes, well you're just following the script.

Sir what is your phone number?

Me: How about I just give you the account number?

I think we can look up your account that way.

{so I rattle off the account number}
{call taker finds my account}

Sir is your ship to address _____?

Me: Yes.

And your billing address _____?

Me: That's correct.

Okay how can I help you?

Me: I would like to order _____

Sir, that is a different department, I will transfer you now.
{1970's disco music plays while on hold}

{Call Taker #2 with a deep smokers voice comes on the line.}
Sir, may I have your name?

Me: For the love of Pete, I already gave the first person my information.

Sir, humor me.

Me: A Priest, A Rabbi and The President walk into a bar.

Sir, I don't understand.

Me: Never mind.

Sir, can I have your name please.
{I give my name}

Sir, that name doesn't show up in my system.

Me: OMG

Sir, I will need to transfer you to another department as your name is not being found.

Me: I don't want to live anymore, just shoot me please.

Sir, I assure the next department can help you.

{Call Taker #3 with a thick foreign accent comes on the line.}

Sir, may I have your name?

Me: NO! I've already told all my information to two other people, go find them and get the notes from them.

Sir, I am in a separate department, on a different floor.

Me: Run Forest Run!

Sir, I don't think you understand the distance between departments.

Me: Does it look like I care at this point.

Sir, what you're asking will take time.

Me: Well I've already spent 10 minutes dealing with idiots so while you are hunting down who you need to talk to I will be water boarding myself to pass the time.

Sir, can I just transfer you to someone else.

Me: Don't you dare.
{beep, beep, beep....click}

He hung up.

Hey Rob, hey Rob, hey Rob...
Me: Hey go be someone else's problem.

About The Author

Rob is a Certified Digital Marketing Strategist, a Foremost Expert On Specialized SEO, a Serial Author, Podcaster, Speaker and Authority Broadcaster who can help amplify YOU to your audience.

Rob has also produced books for many clients including lawyers, doctors, copywriters, speakers and consultants.

Rob helps companies across the globe generate new revenue and capture online business. And he hates scammers with a passion.

Rob is available to share talks and give interviews.

To learn more about Rob visit **AnspachMedia.com** or call Anspach Media at **(412)267-7224** today.

What Makes Me One Of The Foremost Experts On Specialized SEO?

Truth to be told there are thousands of people claiming to do SEO and very few can optimize a website like I do.

Why?

What makes me different?

Besides being the coauthor of "Optimize This" a #1 international best-selling book on SEO (#1 in 4 Countries: USA, CANADA, JAPAN & Australia - #2 in UK, Germany), I've created what's called A.P.E. keyword indexing which allows me to rank websites for 30, 40, 50 or more keywords and phrases and helps my clients websites dominate the search engines.

What is A.P.E. keyword indexing you might be asking?

A.P.E. is an acronym for Analytical, Psychological & Emotional. By using A.P.E. when formulating your SEO, you are ranking your website not for the common industry jargon your competitors are vying for - but for the keywords your exact clients are looking for. By focusing on your visitor's needs, wants, desires, frustrations, and pain you are creating a website that ranks for their specific searches and helps you convert more long term clients. Whereas your competitors are focusing on competing with each other and forgetting the needs of the visitor thus getting a bunch of low converting tire kickers.

So if you're going to invest in SEO, make sure the person you are hiring can rank you for more than the typical industry standard five keywords that most offer. Yes, there are plenty of cheap SEO'ers out there, unfortunately, you get what you pay for and sadly, cheap SEO doesn't equate to attracting and converting the right clientele.

Oh, and to the person who tried to tell me that SEO doesn't take effect until Google decides to index your website - that's absolutely BS. I can optimize a website and in real time see that the changes that have been made. A site that is optimized correctly can start ranking and converting faster. So, if someone tells you it takes months for SEO to work or that you have to wait for Google to decide to index the site, tell them to kick rocks then call me at **(412)267-7224** or send me a chat through the Anspach Media website at www.AnspachMedia.com I'll look over your site, let you know why it's not ranking, and give a quote on improving it.

Resources

THE INTERVIEW SERIES FOR ENTREPRENEURS

Rob Anspach interviews talented entrepreneurs who demonstrate an eagerness to share their experiences, their knowledge and their stories to help others succeed.

Listen to the Rob Anspach's E-Heroes Podcast today.

Available on:

Apple, Google, Himalaya, Stitcher, Spotify, TuneIn

Or

www.AnspachMedia.com

Rob Versus The Scammers

Protecting The World Against Fraud, Nuisance Calls & Downright Phony Scams.

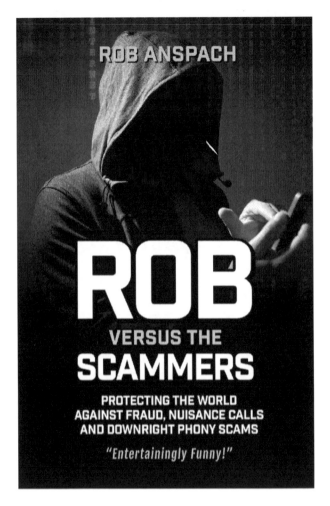

Available on Amazon in Print & Kindle
or at…
www.RobVersusTheScammers.com

Other Books By Rob Anspach

Available on Amazon in Print & Kindle.

www.amazon.com/author/robertanspach

Remember to…

Share This Book!

Share it with your friends!

Share it with your colleagues!

Share it with law enforcement!

Share it on social media.

Share it using this hashtag...

#RobVersusTheMorons

Made in the USA
Columbia, SC
11 October 2022